POEMS WRITTEN THROUGH BARBED-WIRE FENCES

RO MEHROOZ

Poems Written Through Barbed-wire Fences

Translated from the Rohingya by
the author and James Byrne

Introduced by James Byrne

Arc
PUBLICATIONS
2024

Published by Arc Publications,
Nanholme Mill, Shaw Wood Road
Todmorden OL14 6DA, UK
www.arcpublications.co.uk

Copyright in the poems © Ro Mehrooz, 2024
Translation copyright © Ro Mehrooz & James Byrne, 2024
Introduction copyright © James Byrne, 2024
Poetics copyright © Ro Mahrooz, 2024
Copyright in the present edition © Arc Publications 2024

978 1911469-83 4

Design by Tony Ward
Printed in the UK by TJ Books

Cover photograph: 'Contrast' by Ro Mehrooz
© Ro Mehrooz, 2024

This book is in copyright. Subject to statutory exception and to provision of relevant collective licensing agreements, no reproduction of any part of this book may take place without the written permission of Arc Publications.

Arc Chapbook Series
Series Editor: Tony Ward

CONTENTS

Introduction: James Byrne / 9

14 / Raát Kí Rani • Night-Blooming Jasmine / 15
16 / Noó Asé Gór Noó Asé Mon • No, I Don't Have A Home or the Strength To Speak / 17
18 / Rifújí Keémp • Refugee Camp / 19
20 / Hítára Añáré Foráí Féle • They Forget Me / 21
22 / Ofúrání sófor • Endless Journey / 23
24 / Beilor Wada • The Sun's Promise / 25
26 / Ruzar San • Ramadan Moon / 27
28 / Ki Rosóm Faillé Koume • What A Tradition the People Have Embraced / 29
32 / Ek Fiyala Saá Háitó Sáilám • I Wanted A Cup of Tea / 33
34 / Nou Ḍufáyyá Mazí • The Boat-sinking Oarsman / 35
36 / Orghúmá • Insomnia / 37
38 / Doldoli • Quicksand / 39
40 / Hókkor Larái Kamiyab Óibó • The Fight For Truth Will Be Victorious / 41

Poetics: Ro Mehrooz / 42
Biographical Notes / 47

To Nani, my late grandmother,
and to all the Rohingya that are trying to
catch a breath among the never-ending
persecution and miseries of life.

'RO' FOR ROHINGYA: AN INTRODUCTION TO *POEMS WRITTEN THROUGH BARBED-WIRE FENCES*

In this introduction, I am prepared to say only so much about Ro Mehrooz. The reason for this is to protect his safety, the most important condition of our working process and friendship over the last five years. Ro lives under another name in a location I cannot disclose. I know his real name, though I cannot share this either, nor any specific family history or details that might help you get a more complete 'picture' of his life, such as the village he is from. I realise this makes for a somewhat concealed introduction. However, it is written after five years of having never used Ro's real name, just in case the trail of our conversation might cause him any harm.

In 2017, the Tatmadaw (the brutal military majority of the Burmese government) burned down large swathes of land in the Rohingya homeland of Arakan and deliberately killed men (and also women and children), displacing almost a million more. Cox's Bazar refugee camp, on the border of Bangladesh and Myanmar was, for many, the only place to flee to. Close to one million Rohingya live there, in desperate conditions, stateless and in limbo. Some have tried to return home in recent years and, as I write this, few people in the West appear to be paying attention to how the Tatmadaw have, over recent months, once more increased their violence against the Rohingya.[1] Rohingya men are being used as human shields in a war between the Tatmadaw and the Arakan Army (AA), a Buddhist-Rakhine resistance force. Quite literally caught in the crossfire, the Rohingya are also being faced with an impossible ultimatum: be killed or be

---

[1] Few sources are available, but for this recent article in the *Guardian*, published 14 May 2024 (https://www.theguardian.com/global-development/article/2024/may/14/rohingya-being-forcibly-conscripted-in-battle-between-myanmar-and-rebels).

forcibly conscripted to fight on either side. Children are being snatched from their homes to fight and, once again, as with the genocide in 2017, bodies are being found on the streets, and villages are being torched.

'Ro' stands for Rohingya, a fairly common pseudonym for poets I met in the Cox's Bazar refugee camp five years ago, and a defiantly communal gesture against the genocidal operations of the Burmese military. Since first meeting in the camps, Ro and I keep in touch regularly. Among an impressive generation of Rohingya poets[2], Ro is rare in that, these days, he writes mostly in the Rohingya language. This is a way for him to reconnect with his community and culture, despite being separated from it, a kind of survival in and of itself.[3] Ro, still in his twenties, is multilingual; he has also written poems in English, the language many poets I met in Cox's chose to use so they might be more easily heard. Ro's poems in English are exceptionally good; however, we chose not to include these for his debut publication, which represents a milestone, in that it is the first time – at least in modern times – that a collection of Rohingya language poetry has been published in the West.

Given the quality of his work, it is surprising that Ro, at the time I met him, had only just begun to consider writing poetry. He was too busy trying to survive outside of the camps, risking everything to receive the post-school education denied to his people and becoming the first person in his family to attend university. After deciding he wasn't going to live in the camps, his choice was to live in hiding elsewhere, or return to Myanmar. He chose to live in Bangladesh. What must it have been like for Ro, separated from community, friends and family, to live with the fear that his identity, kept secret from others yet so important to him, might, at any time, be discovered? At the very least, Ro

---

[2] See *I Am A Rohingya: Poets from the Refugee Camps and Beyond*, edited by Shehzar Doja & James Byrne (Arc, 2019). This anthology arose from two days of creative writing workshops in Cox's Bazar.
[3] For more on this, read Ro's 'Poetics' at the back of this volume.

would be sent back to the refugee camp. What must it be like to keep looking over your shoulder, wondering if you might be found out for being who you are? I realise, on writing this, that I've never asked Ro these questions and his poetry doesn't necessarily try to answer them. Why should it? In many respects he is simply another key poet of our times, and the quality of his work should be considered in aesthetic terms, according to his abilities in using the artistic palette. The poems in this collection include a range of techniques and styles, familiar to anyone in the West – lyric address, imagery[4], metaphor, Romanticism, linguistic play. They also consistently include activist responses to the genocide and current plight of the Rohingya, though at times this can be subtly implied, via a simple wish to share a cup of tea with a loved one or surviving a fit of insomnia. And yet for all the subtleties in his poetics, the activism remains a stirring undertow in *Poems Written Through Barbed-wire Fences*.

Rohingya is seldom written by Ro's generation and official figures of those who speak the language are never reliable. And yet the language survives, as do its people in a state of precariousness. For years, the Rohingya have fought to publish using their own script, though there is still no accepted written form of the language. About three years ago I became aware of how Ro himself began writing more poems in Rohingya. These appeared a little different from those Arc first published in *I Am A Rohingya* and are not included here, except for 'Night-Blooming Jasmine'. His Rohingya language poems frequently make use of rhyme and metre. As Ro points out in his 'Poetics' (p. 44), traditional Rohingya forms do exist in terms of having distinct names. However, they emanate from a different kind of lineage,

---

[4] In addition to writing poetry, Ro is also an award-winning photographer. His image of a man in the camps staring into a whirlpool of mud (titled 'Lost in Reflection: a Rohingya's Gaze into Hope's Abyss') was featured in the British Museum exhibition, *Burma to Myanmar*.

that of orality, from songs passed down across generations. Back in the camps, Shehzar Doja and I invited Jani Alam, a famous Rohingya folk singer, to sing in front of the poets we workshopped. Many of the songs had been heard by those present, but were often remembered through different versions. Ro, in this collection, is innovative in his use of traditional rhyme and metre, as well as songs or lullabies, expanding his poetic tradition in the process. 'No, I Don't Have A Home or The Strength To Speak', for example, with its 'ki, ki' line-endings, is a newly-invented form. 'Refugee Camp' is a prose poem, still quite rare in Rohingya poetics. These are more explicit examples of poems that stand up to the deadly aggression of the Tatmadaw, but they are also extending a literary tradition that has, like its people, frequently been under threat. In their home of Myanmar, the regime refuses to recognise the Rohingya language. The brutality of the Tatmadaw has not just tried to exterminate a people by physical persecution, but also by cultural and linguistic censorship.

Though we met regularly online, the process of translation has been unhurried. After working up literal translations, with Ro leading (I am not a Rohingya language speaker), we then held meetings on around twenty occasions. Even though literal translations had been made, we would discuss a few stanzas and only sometimes did a poem, even a short poem, feel 'finished' after meetings lasting several hours. As I had come to realize many years before when working with the Burmese language, it is futile to translate word-by-word since both English and Rohingya languages frequently use the sentence in different ways. This echoes what Walter Benjamin stated over a hundred years ago: 'no translation would be possible if in its ultimate essence it strove for likeness to the original'.[5] All poems here involve a reconfiguration of language via translation rather than any

---

[5] Walter Benjamin, 'The Translator's Task', translated by S. Rendall (2012; first published in German in 1923).

absolute mirroring effect. On occasions, we felt a sense of musicality inherent in the host language could be retained and we tried to incorporate this into our process, sounding out poems, trying repeatedly to be faithful to such a complex language as Rohingya appears to be.

As I write this introduction, I am again in touch with Ro. Despite being one of the major voices in Rohingya poetics, he doesn't much feel like writing at the moment. For the past two days he has been worried about whether his remaining family in Myanmar are dead or alive. Rohingya collaborators with the Burmese military were about to take his cousin, a mere boy, as part of the forced conscription, despite knowing he was underage. Ro's uncle was also threatened with conscription. Instead, villages and fields that Ro used to walk through as a boy were burned and his aunt and remaining family have been forced to flee. He waits on news, rumour, hoping they are safe.[6]

Many Rohingya are dying at present and have died throughout history at the hands of the Burmese regime. Here is the voice of a survivor, one of the most exceptional and humane people I have worked with. I hope you might read these poems and enjoy them for their own poetic merits and perhaps, beyond this, think about what you could do to raise awareness that might help his people. As *Poems Written Through Barbed-wire Fences* makes us aware, the Rohingya community has been waiting too long for their basic human rights to be respected.

James Byrne
May 2024

---

[6] Fortunately, at the time of going to press, Ro's family are safe, although the violence against the Rohingya community continues in Myanmar, echoing the lead-up to the genocide of 2018. See https://www.independent.co.uk/asia/south-asia/myanmar-rakhine-genocidal-violence-rohingya-b2574528.html

RAÁT KÍ RANI

O sandá mamu sandá mamu hotá fúnó saí
Fúúddólá roṅg fiñdí muúntú ayó saí
Tuáñllá soiñ táikke raát kí ranir holi
Boyar aibó írír írír holi zaibóí zórí
Uṛán bíṛán aga gura dibo kúṣbó gorí

O sandá mamu sandá mamu hotá fúnó saí
Fúúddólá roṅg fiñdí muúntú ayó saí
Bubu hoyé matát dibo raát kí ranir holi
Fúñtát mazé gañtí gañtí fúlór sórá bañdí
Aró dibó hátot moódí fúáñjjá zérfúáín mili
Dui din bade bubur biyá biyát aibá ní?

O sandá mamu sandá mamu hotá fúnó saí
Fúúddólá roṅg fiñdí biyát ayó saí

NIGHT-BLOOMING JASMINE

This poem is a retelling of a popular lullaby that Rohingya mothers sing to calm their babies, ('O moon, moon…come, come. come / eat rice with milk and banana.'). 'Bubu' means elder sister.

O moon uncle, moon uncle, please hear me.
Come to me wearing white.
For you, the buds of the night-blooming jasmine wait.
The wind will blow, blow gently, the buds will fall.
The whole yard will smell of its scent.

O moon uncle, moon uncle, please hear me.
Come to me wearing white.
Bubu said she will place buds of the night-blooming jasmine
on her head, knitting the threads into a wreath.
She will dye henna on her hands among friends.
Her wedding is in two days, will you come?

O moon uncle, moon uncle, please hear me.
Come to the wedding wearing white.

NOÓ ASÉ GÓR NOÓ ASÉ MON

Noó asé gór noó asé mon asé hoíbár ki ki
Fúnóyá yo hoṛé asé hoyúm haré ki ki

Sensár beráí ṣúka bórí nokót dilám bari
Faássólóí ṭani gibot goillám aro goillám ki ki

Dana besi iman añárá diyí doijjat ḍali
Muúmmíká ayér nosól tarár óíbó ki ki

Bháyé bháyé háná haní fororé loi ṭana ṭani
Ki zindegi geilgóí añrár aró zaibo ki ki

Sukh táí añdá óyyi añárá gal táí buk óyyí
Bēlómí loi mogoz dúye aró dúíbó ki ki

Gujja haṛi mujjáí féille roidot fúaddi
Hoto zala ṣói félailám ṣóoyúm aró ki ki

Noó asé san noó asé tara asé ar ki ki
Zindegit foór asé hoṛé dekhíyúm añí ki ki

Noó asé tór noó asé mon asé hoíbár ki ki
Fúnóyá yo hoṛé asé hoyúm haré ki ki

NO, I DON'T HAVE A HOME OR THE STRENGTH TO SPEAK

No, I don't have a home or the strength to speak. What do I have
                                                          to say, what?
When no-one listens, who do I speak to? What would I say, what?

I rolled the family census paper, heaped with tobacco, tapped
                                                  the filter with a thumbnail.
Took a drag from the *Faássólóí*, gossiped, and did whatever. Whatever.

Selling drugs, we squandered our faith in the river.
What will happen to the next generation, what?

Friendly among strangers, bickering among brothers.
What a life passed us by. What else will pass? What?

Even with eyes, we were blind. Even with a mouth, we were silent.
They washed our brains with illiteracy. What else is to be washed? What?

Root-cut, severed, forced to dry out in the sun.
So much we have suffered. What else is there to suffer? What?

No moon, no stars. What else is there? What?
Is there any light in my life? What can I see? What?

No space underfoot. No strength to speak. What do I have to say, what?
When no-one listens, who do I speak to? What would I say, what?

Note:
Faássólóí is a thin cigarette or mini-cigar filled with tobacco flakes and commonly wrapped in a leaf or paper fixed with adhesive at one end.

RIFÚJÍ KEÉMP

Gelde háttát beşí gorom foijjíl. Duanot uggwá manúṣ koólót hoóddé "añárá jáhánnámór ḍákóttún tákhí dé!". E háttát beşí zór der. Mainşór górór salor woror faníttún nou baí kessú mainşóré zaga lari der. Feésebúk ót dekhílám dé "tuñárá ré māna soil der, tel der, dail der. Tuñáráttún kiyór sinta?" Maik loi ḍak di hoílo dé "Keémp 9 ót haindá bháñgí baf loi fua loi mori giyóy bolé". Héṛe zai saílám dé beṛi uggwá háñdédde, "mazé zailé mazé mare, kule zailé kule mare, mā ré súsuní!".

Mainşé hoódé eṛé tinnwá muúsúm asé – doror muúsúm. Horánnyá oinor ḍor, bariṣá fanír ar haindá bháñgár ḍor, şítkállyá şíté hoilla musorar ḍor. Mazé hálí din táile gulir ḍor.

REFUGEE CAMP

Last week, searing heat. In the shop, a man on a call: 'We live near the hellfire!' This week, heavy rains. People are being moved by boat from water raised above roofs. I saw on Facebook: 'You are given free rice, oil, lentils. What worries do you have left?' A loud announcement from the mic: 'Landslide killed father and son in Camp 9.' Arriving there, a woman wails: 'the centre beats me if I go to the centre, the shore beats me if I go to the shore. O mother, mermaid!'

Here, people say there are three seasons – seasons of fear. Fear of fire in the summer, fear of floods and landslides in the monsoon, the heart-wrenching fear of winter. And, if there are any days left, the fear of bullets in between.

HÍTÁRA AÑÁRÉ FORÁÍ FÉLE

Lamba lamba gulir ḍoillá kemera loi ayé
Ze guli loi meleṭéríyé añár mā baf guṣṣí mari féláyé
Añáré foṭú mare
Keñṛa taror baátún táí maré
Añí honó sirahánár januwaronnán!
Añí honó bak noó hoñittam
Azara háf noó beráítám
Honó zala de bāndor noó
Añí uggwá insán nóní?
Keñṛa taror bútóré aí maré
Tarár hóbór lekhé
Ham óílé fiṭ di zagóí
Har monot hone rakhé
Hítára añáré foráí féle

THEY FORGET ME

> *After escaping rape and being burnt alive during the Tula Toli massacre in August 2017, Mumtaz Begum was interviewed by international media where she said, 'I want justice and I want to tell the world all the things the military did. They raped and killed us. We want justice.' After years of waiting for justice, Mumtaz appears to be hopeless and fed up with seemingly inconsequential interviews by the press. In an interview with my friend, she says, 'Once they collect the information, they never contact me.'*

Long, long, gun-like, they come with cameras,
guns with which the military killed my family.
They photograph me
across the barbed-wire fence,
as if I am a zoo animal!
I am not a tiger that bites,
not a python that strangles,
not some irritable monkey.
Am I not a human?
They come inside the barbed-wire fence, photograph me,
write their reports.
When their work is finished, they turn back and go.
Who remembers who?
They forget me.

OFÚRÁNÍ SÓFOR

Oñṣṣá rait hoto lamba
Gā matá ím, sukhót ghúm no ayé
Áñṛilám boót duré
Ajjó monzil hañsé no ayé
Aṣá diló rait fúrar hoí
Ratá kurár bak funá no ayé
Bajjailám hoto doroda
Ajjó honó juwab no ayé

Holiddwá fúl bointe deháza
Háráyá hók keén fírí no ayé?
Fúinnidé foór bole hókkolór beṣ sole
Añár híkka kén ebbereo no ayé?
Áñṛilám boót duré
Ajjó monzil hañsé no ayé

ENDLESS JOURNEY

Although a more classical approach to form inspires 'Endless Journey', it attempts to break away from the traditional meter. However, the second line of the poem rhymes with every other line via the word 'ayé', which means come or arrive, but is also used as a spoken phrase along with another word. Depending on the context and preceding word, the meaning of the 'ayé' can change. In the Rohingya language, the word order is frequently different from that of English (Subject-Object-Verb), which made it difficult to rhyme the translation, whilst trying to be faithful to the original meaning. Additionally, 'buds cannot be seen when they transform into flowers' is a common Rohingya saying and Oñṣṣá night refers to the longest night of the year.

How dark Oñṣṣá night is!
Cold-bodied, sleep doesn't come close.
I have walked so far,
still the destination is no closer.
They gave me hope the night would end,
the crowing of the rooster was not heard.
I've knocked on so many doors,
still no answer has arrived.

Even buds are visible, transforming into flowers.
Again, why can't lost rights return?
I've heard it is light that travels the fastest,
but why does the light never come my way?
I've walked so far,
still the destination is no closer.

BEILOR WADA

Wada mozin beínná uṛé
Gaíllár múkhót roid fore

Ghúm gas zehón seton ó
Gasór agat báttwá nase

Gom fuain moktobot za
Gaíllá zehón dat añsé

Ṭáṛa fáṛá roid fore
áíllá hakku kér basé

duúñjjá óílé fara nizám
Kírkíríttun roid gólé

Beilor ṣóṛákót dúil nase
Zeiñlla honó tal fúné

Duré honnát fiñyajja gan gaár
añdá dúilór tale tale

Beil no deílé ghúm gas zúré
áñzzua zúrá lesá dóré

Beil zagói oinna mullúk
Foór foóñsá góré góré

Beil hono din ṣúṭkí no lo
Tarfor din házír wadar ore

Wada mozin beínná uṛé
Gaíllár múkhót roid fore

THE SUN'S PROMISE

As promised, rising in the morning,
sunlight falls upon the lazy man's face.

When the sleep-tree wakes up,
Myna birds dance the upper branches.

Virtuous children go to school
while the lazy man scratches his teeth.

Sunlight falls, scorches.
A farmer uncle weeds grasses.

At noon, the village is serene,
sunlight climbs through the window –

particles dance in the light,
as if they can hear music.

Far off, a sparrow sings
to the rhythm of blind atoms.

If the sleep-tree cannot see the sun, it drowses.
The dusk-dozy man copycats,

and the sun travels across provinces,
carrying its light inside every house.

The sun never takes a day off.
As promised, it appears the next day.

As promised, rising in the morning,
sunlight falls upon the lazy man's face.

RUZAR SAN

Ajja ruzar san uṛíbó fara guñguwar
Ruzar kúṣi dilot sáí zai duniya foór foór lār
Gura juwan ekku fúñáti san saitó zar
Fata hoṣṣa haindá baí baí uṛér bainnar faár
San uṛíté deri asé kessú duanot zar
Guñṛa maṣ ruza táíbo ziín ziín azzu hár
Fura bosór azzu goré woktó lamba óító
San no deílé dórforáddé ṭani tuiltó saár

Moiror azan dibar age san uṛíló
San uíṭṭé hoí bóḍḍa abas Mayyú fúnílo
Bosórór dúṣṣá rong hora oí duniya foór óiló

Bideṣót ar noya sanor kúṣi asé hoṛé
Sukhór fání bái zárgói fuñsóyá hon hoṛé

RAMADAN MOON

Ramadan moon will rise today, villages echoing.
Ramadan delight, heart-spread; the world appears illumined.
Together, children and adults go moon-watching.
Teenagers climb up the slopes of Bainna's mountain.
The moon is yet to rise, some stroll towards the shops,
eat whatever they want to, fast a whole month.
Through the year, a wish that time may be stretched.
When the moon can't be seen, anxious, they want to pull it back in.

The moon has risen before the Adhan of Maghrib.
Mayyu heard a loud cheer, 'the moon rises!'
The pale year radiates, a world illumined.

Where is the happiness of a new moon in another's land?
Tears fall down, who is there to wipe them away?

Notes:
Bainnar faár: A mountain in Arakan.
Adhan: A Muslim call to prayer.
Maghrib: The time after the sunset.
Mayyu: A frontier district in Arakan.

KI ROSÓM FAILLÉ KOUME

Ki rosóm faillé koume
Şóróm háyá féille hoṛé
Biyá şádír mamalat tará
Sámánár keñṛa gil mari raikké
Siyú óité asmali mage
"Şágúáng gasor falong hoṛé?"
Di no faillé hotár fúñṭ loi
Gola ṭani dak bórái dé
Goribpyar hasti náidé
Hálot zai záf dí morer
Tar zérfua biş hái morer
Ki rosóm faillé koume
Şóróm hayá féille hoṛé

Biyá şádí ailé tará
Mela gorí şódórí goré
Raitta boí hádíyá gone
Gunárí háilé afsús goré
Arailla farailla byaggún mili
Bowór feṭir hor súlé
Súlí nófáillé bonnair ḍúl
Farar muá muá baze
Ki rosóm faillé koume
Şóróm hayá féille hoṛé

Hóorór górót şántí hoṛé
Sámánár fisálí súre hoṛé
Sámáná dilé gommúá noó hoí
Aité zaité sútá dóré
Baforóttún ṭiñá aintó
Zamai hóorí kilaí mare
Ki rosóm faillé koume
Kuran hádís féille hoṛé

WHAT A TRADITION THE PEOPLE HAVE EMBRACED

What a tradition the people have embraced.
Where have they thrown shame?
In matters of weddings, they
trellis dowry thorns,
asking for clay pot to cupboard:
'what about the teak bed frame?'
If it can't be afforded, they smear
with words of mud.
The poor man, resourceless,
jumps to his death in the sea,
his daughter dies drinking poison.
What a tradition the people have embraced.
Where have they thrown shame?

If there's a wedding, they
arrange banquets, do business.
At night, they sit and count gifts,
regret if they make a loss.
Every villager gathers,
snatches clothes from the bride's case.
If they can't, drums of denigration
echo from the mouth of every village.
What a tradition the people have embraced.
Where have they thrown shame?

Where's peace at the in-law's house?
After the dowry, do they ever stop coming?
If the dowry is given, they say it's a fake,
find fault with every coming and going.
To bring money from the parents' house,
the husband and mother-in-law torment.
What a tradition the people have embraced.
Where have they thrown the Qur'an and Hadith?

Biyá şádí kúşir rosóm
Ayyó beggún ekku fúñáti
Ze manúş sámánár lalsí
Tarloi sírí egana goti
Gozzóppya rosómóttún
Sírí añárá sómájór rosí

Marriage: a tradition of happiness.
Let's step forward together.
Whoever is greedy about dowries,
cut ties with them.
Let's cut the social rope
from this cursed tradition.

EK FIYALA SAÁ

Tuñár fuñáti boí ek fiyala saá háitó saílám
Rong hora, siní beṣí, miṛá háitó saílám

Beñha rasta fiṛót gorí loi giyóy añáré tulí
Duré zaigóy uzu rasta tuwai nó farí

Tuñár fuñáti boí ek fiyala saá háitó saílám
Rong hora, siní beṣí, gorom háitó saílám

Saá fata, siní ar gorur dud añáí annilam
Zaite zaite ṭaimor tonkis gorom hái nó faillám

Ketélíttún goli fori nifí gíyóy tuñṣór sulá
Tokdiror najjol foñsa asé ṣúde mala

Tuñár fuñáti boí ek fiyala saá háitó saílám
Rong hora, siní beṣí, miṛá háitó saílám

Uñṛót mazé fiyala lagai bazái raító saílám
Kismotor háwá mū fíráye ki goríúm añáí

Ṣítkál, kúwa, guzori giyóy saá hái nó faillám
Ekka háñṣi, goppi sóppí mari no faillám

I WANTED A CUP OF TEA

I wanted to sit with you and drink a cup of tea,
a strong, sugared, sweet tea.

The curved road carried me off on its back.
But being so far away, I couldn't find the straight path.

I wanted to sit with you and drink a cup of tea,
a strong, sugared, hot tea.

I brought tea leaves, sugar and cow's milk,
but, en-route, short of time, I couldn't drink it hot.

Because the kettle leaked, the husk stove turned off;
decayed coconut of my fate; only its shell is left.

I wanted to sit with you and drink a cup of tea,
a strong, sugared, sweet tea.

I wanted to keep the cup touching my lip,
but fate's wind turned its face. What can I do?

Winters and mists passed. To drink my tea, I couldn't.
A giggle, a little chit-chat, I couldn't.

NOU ḌUFÁYYÁ MAZÍ

Soiddó dinna sañdor foórót giyyé ḍuli dórí
Hál farayyá háñṛi giló zaga dui ek kuni

Bowór bóíné háñṣi háñṣi, maijjé añiṛá faní
Fúu hóorí yé dójje hóoñlá, gayyé rok dórí

Razar zérfúá bou banayyé, anér bonnout gorí
Tal bazoya bunzaáñz bazar, kiyé marer tali

Tánḍa boyar uñrai loizar, sañdot mazé bari
Mazí ṭaner foñi fuñhayya, hírár fúṛá zórí

Golot ṭane hálor gúlát, nou giló góí ḍufí
Biṣáyá fúl mozi zargóí zaáñlámátár hári

THE BOAT-SINKING OARSMAN

In the custom of Rohingya weddings, a procession begins from the groom's house, which consists of the groom's family and their relatives, and goes to the bride's house. As they arrive at this house, the younger siblings or cousins often throw water to tease the guests. Hóoñlá is a traditional Rohingya wedding song. 'Fúu hóorí' is the auntie-in-law [in this case, of the groom]. She is usually the primary entertainer of the female section in the house. Depending on the situation, she adjusts the lyrics of hóoñlá to tease the bride or her family. If the bride's family has a hóoñlá singer from their side, she too adjusts the lyrics and sings the song, responding to the groom's party. At the end, the pageant returns to the groom's house as they bring the bride home. Zááñlámátá is a dock on the banks of the Mayyu River.

Full moon night, a wedding procession
crosses the river, walks a few acres.

The bride's sister throws dirty water, smiles.
The auntie-in-law sings, Hóoñlá hits a nerve.

Princess made bride, she is brought on a boat.
Musicians tap cymbals, others clap their hands.

A cool breeze wafts rhythm to the moon.
The oarsman pulls hurriedly, diamond drops fall.

A false move and he sinks the boat in a whirlpool.
Flowers spread and rot through *Zááñlámatá*.

ORGHÚMÁ

Bişánót ḍák bodollí ghúm uddya sukh
Ghóñṛír keñṛa loi zibbat der duddufar de buk
Baárkúlé fuñhai boyar aşşé ṭáarór gubbar
Gulap fúlót ṭáṛal foijjé zoler oinor faár
Ṭoin mater ṭón ṭón, kírkíríttun góille şíṭká
Hátot foillo hoek şíṭká keñş waá óiló atíkká
Kíyálor myúlá goillé júm júm dilot laiggé ím
Hombol beráí relíñgót boí gailám deşór git
Ṭáṛal máilló dehá giló kúñş ábujjá rasta
Fanír zibbat dui naláttún hañsat balur bostá
Fanír wóré báşi ailó dui habosor buṭ
Mazí sárá buṭ dekhí dile hoíló uṭ
Dilor giróstí hotá mainní foñyor kíyál náí
Fuhañyya fanít fola buṭ, buṭor súán náí
Ḍufí báşi ailám bideş şántír kúñş o náí?
Şántí dé no ailó fúñáti kúñş hoṛé fair

INSOMNIA

Tossed and turned over in my bed, sleep-stripped eyes,
my chest palpitates, competes with the clock's hands.
Outside, wind-rapid, a cloud of memory arrives –
lightning strikes the rose, a volcano erupts,
ton-ton goes the tin-roof. Through the window, raindrops,
a few drip over my hand, and, suddenly, I get goosebumps –
a cloud of memories melt, *jhum-jhum*, my heart feels cold.
Blanket-wrapped, I sit on the balcony, sing the song of my homeland.
Thunder strikes. Vision of a road with un-wiped footprints,
water racing down the drains, banked with sandbags,
water, on which two floating paper boats arrive.
Seeing the boat without a captain, the heart says 'climb'.
Heart's the master, I listened, but forgot the oars.
A wild boat on speedy water, rudderless.
Drowning and floating, I arrive in another country, no trace of peace.
Where do I find the sign? Peace has not followed me.

DOLDOLI

Duniya yaán doldoli
Zeṛé tíyailám golti gorí
Nasilám kúşi gorí
Aste aste gólílam bói húñş háráí
Zeéné ar uṛí no farí
Honikké tuló more ṭani!

QUICKSAND

The world is quicksand.
By mistake, it's where I stood,
where, ecstatically, I danced.
Slowly, slowly, unconsciously, I sank
so much, I can no longer get out.
Somebody get me out!

HÓKKOR LARÁÍ KAMIYAB ÓÍBÓ

Óh mor téta háyyá afsús wala dil
Zulúm loi berí báindá tor ga azad óíbó
Tor şóppón okkól fura goríbó
Ar hoek din boddaşor ḑúk fií há
Ar hoek din...
Balur góñŗít zulúmór balu nise fori zargóí
Ar ekká gorí basi asé dé...
Fura furi goli zailói góñŗí ar no ulḑibó, añrá no ulḑailé
E Zulúm hámişállá andár gúlát ḑufí zaibóí

Óh mor téta háyyá afsús wala dil
Mui hoí farom tor duk koumor wore nozor şíŗíle
Juan lal hoila okkol golot zagat zoli sáí óí zargóí dé dekhílé
Fúlór holi okkol rong dúí dúşşá óí zárgóí dé dekhílé
Lékín, mehénnótór miyúlá asmanor zoñlot sáí giyóy
Joldi kamiyabir zórór fúŗá ókkól fori fúlór holit rong aníbó

Óh mor téta háyyá afsús wala dil
Mui hoí farom tor duk insánór áñḑḑí kuiñre sabadde dekhílé
Meleţérír gulit laşór faár dekhílé
nalár beng lowót háñsúréddé dekhílé
Lékín, kamiyabir ḑól bái ayér
Añárá tin oñlor sálámí loi
Zat, dhórmó, samor rong, maya morodor dhair búzáí
Zalemor khéláf laráí goríddé hétólla
Hókkor laráí kamiyab óíbó

THE FIGHT FOR TRUTH WILL BE VICTORIOUS

> *Written after the coup d'état in my home country, Myanmar, in 2021 when I was in the confinement of my room in another's country during the coronavirus lockdown, this poem is a consolation to me in a state of solitude. During the time, seeing countless protesters being violently attacked and killed, I was trying to contemplate what it would mean for the country and my community's fate as the brutal Tatmadaw regime, who committed genocidal atrocities against my people, grabs power again.*

Oh, my bruised, sad heart,
Your body, oppressively shackled, will be free.
Your dreams will be fulfilled,
a few more days. Drink gulps of patience.
A few more days…
In the hourglass, the sand of tyranny falls down.
Just a few more days left…
If sifted, the hourglass will not overturn (if we don't turn it).
This tyranny will sink into a black hole forever.

Oh my bruised, sad heart,
I know your pain spreading its gaze upon the people,
when you see young red coals burn to ashes for the wrong cause,
when you see flower buds turn pale.
Still, toil clouds spread the sky's nest.
Soon, victory's raindrops will fall on the buds and revive colour.

Oh my bruised, sad heart,
I know your pain when you see dogs chew human bones,
when, through a soldier's gun, you see mountains of corpses,
when you see gutter frogs swimming in blood.
Still, the flood-tide of victory rolls forward,
raising a three-fingered salute,
removing lines of ethnicity, religion, skin colour, woman, man.
Because we fight against tyrants,
the fight for truth will be victorious.

POETICS

Fearing arbitrary arrest and a bleak future, I smuggled myself across the border fence to Bangladesh seven days before my sixteenth birthday. I did not know how long or far this journey would take me from my homeland, Arakan. Previously, the longest time I had stayed away from home was nine days – culturally we stay with our parents. I could not bring many things for this journey beyond what I carried in my mind.

My time in Bangladesh was getting ever longer. The hope of returning home was marred by events such as genocidal crackdowns on my Rohingya people by the Tatmadaw in 2016 and 2017, border tensions and fear of getting tipped off to the police if I returned.[7] I was growing impatient and my energy had to be released before it exploded. Before leaving Myanmar, I had only completed 10th grade. So I wasn't exposed to different experiences beyond what my small town, with its imposed restrictions on movement, had to offer.

Growing up, I used to love drawing in the empty pages of my notebooks, the spaces in my textbooks, and even on walls, for which I was often admonished by my parents. By the end of my school years, I acquired a laptop and thought I could do something related to computing, but was not sure exactly what this might be. I didn't grow up reading books – something that's not prevalent among my people to whom even going to school is a privilege – except books in non-native languages, for example Burmese and English, that were forced upon me during class. Therefore, writing was not one of the ways I had envisioned to transform my ever-growing energy. Instead I was listening to regional music and hearing stories of Jafar Kawal, a Rohingya revolutionary poet. It was around this

---

[7] The Immigration Department photographs Rohingya households every year to keep track of the population. If a member fails to appear in the photograph, he or she will be removed from the household list, making making that person's existence illegal in the country.

time I wrote my first ever poem which began:

> We are Bulbuls of Arakan
> Where shall we go, leaving this garden?

I subsequently wrote a couple more poems which were lost. They were not meant to be read by others, partly because composing poems was, until recently, stigmatised in my culture. Those who do so are considered to be in a romantic relationship, or heartbroken, both of which are also taboos. Even if my people write occasional poems, they often keep them to themselves. However, a community of young poets is breaking free from these taboos[8].

Rohingya is largely an oral language without an established writing system. It is not recognised as an official language by Myanmar, which also stripped the citizenship of its speakers by a law in 1982 that has underpinned decades of persecution. This has impeded efforts to standardise and establish a writing system for the language. In fact, when first learning about Jafar Kawal, I could not read or listen to his poems because they were passed down orally as with other works of literature in my language. No recordings were available to me either.

So, gradually, when I started channelling my emotions and experiences into poetry, I began a quest of understanding how to write poems properly. I began to read poets like Robert Frost, Khalil Gibran, Ezra Pound, and other poems translated into English on the internet, since books were not easily accessible. But I mostly read poems in Urdu from the Rekhta Foundation's website[9]. I wrote a few poems in English and Urdu, only to realise that I was translating my thoughts from the Rohingya language into languages I am not fluent enough in. Around this time, I took a vow to write in my native tongue so as to be able to express my thoughts more fully. Not only

---

[8] Examples of this can be found in *I Am a Rohingya* (Arc, 2019) but also in collections recently published by Rohingya writers found in this anthology, or in works published online.
[9] https://rekhta.org/

did I take this decision for my own convenience (to write in a language more comfortably), but because several other factors guided me towards it. For example, when I encouraged my peers to write in the Rohingya language, some of them found the 'writing' aspect difficult, although not because of a lack in their understanding of the language. It was more the idea that writing creatively was still untried and unfamiliar. When compared to other, established literatures, Rohingyas have very few written materials available in their language that they can take inspiration from. I felt a sense of responsibility to lead by example. The displacement of the majority of the speakers of my language from their homeland has seen them adopt local languages of host countries that have, to some degree, mutual intelligibility. This places the Rohingya language in danger of extinction, and has also pushed me to write in the language for its revival and survival. I consciously include sayings and alternative synonyms in my poems, where they fit, for their preservation, such as *mazé zailé mazé mare* (the centre beats me if I go to the centre), *kule zailé kule mare* (the shore beats me if I go to the shore), *mā ré súsuní!* (O mother, Mermaid), *roid* (sunlight), *ṣóṛák* (sun-ray), *áñzzua zúrá* (dusk-dozy man), *siyú* (large clay pot) and *tuñṣór sulá* (husk stove).

Rohingya poems have been composed for ears. Music and rhymes have been, and remain, an integral feature. This too has been an element of my poetics since a Rohingya readership is still not widespread, although I believe this is on course to change. However, as things are, a lack of readership poses challenges when writing in forms that require visual markers such as punctuation. When studying surviving oral poems, such as 'Bákúm Bákúm Kiñárá' (The Chomping Crab), 'Asmanor Tara' (Stars of the Sky), 'Furma Hálót Diyo' (Ghost in the Furma River) and 'Ilíṣ masór tiríṣ keñṛa' (Thirty Bones of Hilsa Fish). I realised traditional forms – such as *fod* (verse), *futí* (epic poem), *bilak* (elegy), *zari* (lament), *hóoñlá* (wedding song)[10] – have particular metrical and rhyming schemes.

---

[10] Rohang King, 'The Art Garden', *Rohingya Anniversary Magazine* No. 1, p.108

They are mostly composed of couplets, sometimes presenting nostalgic beauty and connecting readers with missing links in Rohingya literature and history, but also placing constraints on getting the most out of the language. Therefore, I have not shied away from experimenting with different forms and techniques, such as free verse, metaphors, words, phases, and so on. For example, 'decayed coconut of my fate; only its shell is left' (p. 33), 'black hole' (p. 41), 'The Fight For Truth Will Be Victorious' (p. 41) are metaphors or unusual phrases that challenge readers' expectations, new words, and written in new forms that I have experimented with for the first time in the Rohingya language.

'No, I Don't Have A Home or The Strength To Speak' (p. 17) is a poem that encapsulates my poetics. It is inspired by a song I was listening to entitled 'Dost'[11] by Abida Parveen, where the first line ends with *Kya Ky*a (which means 'what what' in Urdu), I started the poem with *ki ki* (also meaning 'what, what' in Rohingya). I composed the poem in a traditional form similar to *Duwarai Fod* (Repetitive Versification) with couplets, yet also with experimental metrical structures and inventive rhyming scheme. Thematically, the poem captures the current realities faced by my Rohingya community. It contemplates the present and a future that awaits us. It also looks back at the decades-long persecution the Rohingya have endured, such as the systemic restrictions on education and its consequences.

Although Jafar Kawal was an initial inspiration, as mentioned, I have also been influenced by many poets, both known and previously unknown to me: among others, James Byrne, with his years-long guidance through poetry exchanges and translation sessions; Dunya Mikhail with her 'Tablets'; the Rohingya activist poet Yar Tin; Ahmed Faraz; and, particularly, Faiz Ahmed Faiz with his remarkable ability to expand the conventional thematic expectations of traditional Urdu forms, such as the Ghazal, to encompass

---

[11] http://bit.ly/4d0774T

political and social issues.

Apart from literary influences, I have also been influenced by photography, music, films and other visual art forms. As a practising photographer, I often write my lines as individual scenes or footages and then stitch them into a poem – a film – that tells a story. Usually, I achieve this using imagery, a technique I learned from attending my first-ever poetry workshop with Byrne and Shehzar Doja in Cox's Bazar refugee camp.

I write poems to explore the literary scope of the Rohingya language. Although it is a language I learned as my mother tongue, I was not allowed to study it formally and remained ignorant of its beauty and capabilities until beginning to write these poems. By using my own language, I try to reconnect with memories of home, identity and history of my Rohingya community that are continually suppressed by attempts to erase its existence. I write to illustrate the ongoing hardships and struggles of my community. My primary objective in writing is to document my language, literature and culture as a form of resistance against their disappearance, so that these words can be passed down to the next generation.

The next poem I would like to write is simply a 'poem'. I have not been able to compose much poetry lately, even if I wanted to. Atrocities against my community continue, even as I write this. I am not sure if writing a poem will immediately change the path of the bullet before it hits my brother. If I write of a magical house, will it provide shelter for those people hiding in the fields after their houses are burned? I remain unsure if writing will provide any immediate remedy for the suffering of my people, because that has always been an objective of mine – to write as a form of activism and advocacy for my community. But, seeing the worsening circumstances of my people, at some point I begin to doubt if writing can be the best form of activism for matters that require urgent attention. How to draw attention to the fact that my people are still dying? Until I find answers to these questions, I, as a storyteller, will have to find ways to tell my stories, and the story of my community, in various shapes and forms.

Ro Mehrooz
June 2024

BIOGRAPHICAL NOTES

Ro MEHROOZ is a young Rohingya poet, translator and award-winning photographer. Born in 1999, he is originally from Arakan (now Rakhine State), Myanmar. Growing up under the oppression of Burmese regime, he fled his country at the age of sixteen, avoiding arbitrary arrests. Primarily in Rohingya, he started writing in early 2016 about the longing of his homeland and harsh conditions his community face. His poems were published for the first time in 2019 in *I Am A Rohingya: Poetry from the Camps and Beyond*, (Arc Publications, 2019) and various other anthologies and magazines. One of his photographs was featured at the British Museum exhibition 'Burma to Myanmar' in 2023.

JAMES BYRNE is a poet, editor, translator and visual artist. His most recent poetry collection is *The Overmind* (Broken Sleep Books, 2024). Other collections include *Places you Leave* (2022) and *The Caprices* (2019), both with Arc. A *Selected Poems, Nightsongs for Gaia*, is due in early 2025.

In 2012, Byrne co-translated and co-edited *Bones Will Crow* (Arc), the first anthology of contemporary Burmese poetry to be published in English and in 2019 *I Am A Rohingya*, the first book of Rohingya refugee poems in English appeared, also from Arc.

Byrne is the International Editor for Arc Publications and co-editor of *Atlantic Drift: An Anthology of Poetry and Poetics* (Edge Hill University Press/Arc, 2017).